"Naturally painted by Nature Herself"

Ric J. Steininger
photographic artist

"An impression of the great Australian Landscape"

Produced by:

Ric J. Steininger - Publications Pty Ltd

ABN: 34 335 605 933

Post: PO Box 12269, Cairns DC, Queensland 4870 Australia

Tel: 07 4052 1533 (int. +617 4052 1533)

Fax: 07 4031 3688 (int. +617 4031 3688)

Email: ric@steininger.com.au

Web: www.steininger.com.au

Ric J. Steininger - Gallery

Visit: Ric J. Steininger photographic art gallery at

63 Abbott Street (cnr Spence), Cairns City

or visit my website on: **www.steininger.com.au**

Photography, text and design by Ric J. Steininger

Published September 2002

Copyright © 1992 - 2006 Ric J. Steininger

ISBN 0-9581633-0-8   All rights reserved

Printed in China

Assistance with poetry: Tom MacPartland and Maggie Pinkney

Photographed by Brad Newton

"Welcome to my gallery"

An Introduction

The image "Little Upolu" (next page) is dedicated to my wife, Michiko, who was with me for most of the time whilst working on this collection. It is also a symbol of her patience and support.

As a youngster who enjoyed exploring and travelling to new and special places, I developed a passion for photography that affected everything that I did, it changed my career and kept me moving till I was able to finally settle down in Cairns, Australia.

I first set out to photograph for the arts in 1992 when I left to travel throughout Japan. I was 24 years old. I had just sold everything that I owned and purchased a heavy, bulky panoramic camera. I travelled to Japan for many reasons (a dream since I was young) but photography was a good excuse. In a way, that is what photography became for me; a good excuse to get out and look for new things and to spend time in places that I found. At the same time, I enjoyed the exposure to life itself, to people, to the land and the sea and to my search for the truths of life.

"Just another day at work!"

I opened my first gallery in 1997, after three years of photographing and another two financing. With a love for colour, composition, character and the inspiring; I live in search for that special location. I now have a collection of artistic pieces which not only touch my soul but also, I hope, will touch yours. Photography in recent years has become a more accepted form of art, and to me true art is always defined as a dedication to sculpting a form that touches and inspires the soul.

Ric J. Steininger

"The wise man travels to discover himself"

James Lowell

Film: 100ASA transparency   **Exposure:** 4 seconds   **Filtering:** none   **Time/conditions:** sunset

"Desert Oaks"

Uluṟu-Kata Tjuṯa National Park - World Heritage Area, Central Australia

"Spinifex"

Uluṟu-Kata Tjuṯa National Park - World Heritage Area, Central Australia

The magnificent Uluṟu (Ayers Rock) standing tall in a sea of spinifex grass as the early morning sun splashes across their tops.

The spinifex grass is found widely in Central Australia especially in the heart where Uluṟu and Kata Tjuṯa stand. It is a hardy grass surviving the heat of the summers and the cold of the winter nights as well as the fires that periodically come through. The spinifex grass is the food source for many small wildlife and insects. Aborigines for generations have used the resin from the spinifex grass to make their spears and various instruments. The resin is extracted from the spinifex through heat and has strong adhesive properties.

Above:
Both Uluru (Ayers Rock) and Kata Tjuta (Olgas) where captured in the full moon at dusk light, 20 minutes after sunset.
The gentle dusk light shows up the warmth and beautiful forms of these two monoliths as they stand alone in the vastness of the Central Australia desert. The contours, lines and shades are complimented in this special light.

"The best remedy for those who are afraid, lonely or unhappy is to go outside, somewhere where they can be quite alone with the heavens, nature and God"

Anne Frank

Film: 100ASA transparency   **Exposure:** 4 seconds   **Filtering:** none   **Time/conditions:** sunrise

"Hand of God"
Uluṟu-Kata Tjuṯa National Park - World Heritage Area, Central Australia

Kata Tjuṯa

Uluṟu-Kata Tjuṯa National Park - World Heritage Area, Central Australia

The rich red glow on the horizon, red and yellow dusk with the black of the night sky and in the presence of Kata Tjuṯa (Olgas).

Film: 50 ASA transparency   **Exposure:** 20 seconds   **Filtering:** none   **Time/conditions:** 45 minutes after sunset

Previous page:

"Hand of God"
Uluru (Ayers Rock), Central Australia

The open horizon of Central Australia shows the huge, impressive Ayers Rock as just a thumb nail on the vast horizon.

I was trying to photograph Kata Tjuta one morning from a particular angle, but it was not working out very well because the cloud on the horizon was covering the early morning sun. But what I saw on the horizon was much more spectacular. The massive Uluru was just a small bump silhouetted against the vast open horizon with shafts of the early morning sunlight shining like fingers through the cloud. There was also some fine whisks of rain falling. It was a most moving sight, a lovely experience ... *"Hand of God"*.

Kata Tjuta
Photographed at sunrise

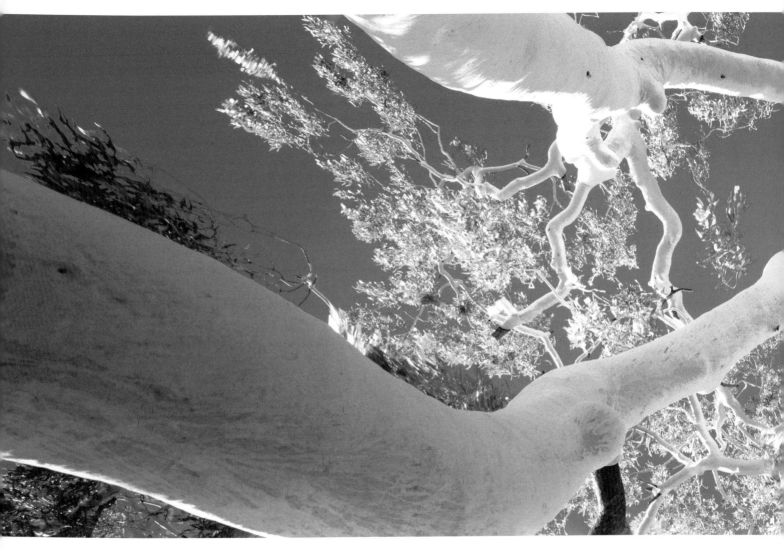

"Separated but united, like lovers entwined"

Tom MacPartland

Film: 100 ASA transparency   **Exposure:** 2 seconds   **Filtering:** none   **Time/conditions:** mid-morning

"We Are One"
Ghost Gums of Ruby Gorge, Alice Springs Central Australia

Film: 50ASA transparency   **Exposure:** 6 hours 24 minute   **Filtering:** none   **Time/conditions:** Stars: from 9:30pm. Sunset: taken two days later over the ocean, on the same frame

"Southern Cross"
A six hour exposure of the night sky, Central Australia

Previous page:

"Southern Cross"
A six hour exposure of the night sky

I had to become a bit of an astronomer during the preparation and photographing of "Southern Cross". It was an enjoyable challenge.

Using a compass as a guide I positioned the camera facing due south. My camera has a 90° view from the horizon to the sky directly above. I waited until 9pm when the Southern Cross and the Pointers moved into full view and then I opened the shutter. Six and a half hours later I closed it again. During the exposure the stars travelled across the sky creating a circular motion, with an unbelievable and unexpected variety of colour.

The Celestial South Pole: If you can imagine standing on the South Pole looking straight up, all the stars would be moving around in circles. This circular motion is visible all the way to the equator.

Two days later I re-exposed the film to a sunset over the ocean.

"All alone in a place of wide wide spaces
man finds his soul"

Ric J. Steininger

Film: 50ASA transparency   **Exposure:** 1 second   **Filtering:** none   **Time/conditions:** sunrise

"Spacious"
On the border of NSW and SA

The desert colours, where the rich blue sky meets the red desert sand and the horizon colours rest on an endless flat expanse.
Spending quite a bit of time in the desert areas was an immense experience. The lack of everything except space and the blue sky. I particularly like the different shades of colour at dusk and dawn, mauve and yellow graduating to the blue sky. I really wanted to capture all of this but felt that it needed something else to connect with, a human touch ... *"Spacious"*.

Film: 100ASA transparency   **Exposure:** 1/2 second   **Filtering:** none   **Time/conditions:** sunrise

"Foot Steps"

The brilliant rich red of the Simpson Desert, Central Australia

"Still Waiting"
In the middle of nowhere, N.S.W. and S.A. Border

Film: 100 ASA transparency   **Exposure:** 2 seconds   **Filtering:** none   **Time/conditions:** sunset

The pink glow on the horizon always rises as the sun goes down.

This land can be so isolated. On a dirt track road with no through traffic, no-one on their way to anywhere. The track that I am on eventually connects with another track that leads to Australia's largest lake, Lake Eyre, which is 70m below sea level and bone dry.

I carried food for 10 days, with 100 litres of water and fuel to travel 1500km. In two days I didn't pass a single car. The weather though was not hot at all compared to the 38° that it reached only a few weeks before. Summer was almost here, but it waited for me.

A fellow by the name of Jack lived in this bus with his verandah, his water and a shady garden - the only trees for 50km. Working on this photograph, the trees seemed to me like people waiting for the bus that never arrived eventually turning into trees ... *"Still Waiting"*.

Previous Page:

"Foot Steps"

The brilliant rich red of the Simpson Desert at dawn, with the soft early morning light gently touching over the landscape. Evidence of the footsteps of lizards and a dingo as they pass by; until the next breeze comes.

"Tropical Vibrance"
Four Mile Beach Port Douglas, Far North Queensland

Film: 50 ASA transparency   **Exposure:** 20 seconds   **Filtering:** none   **Time/conditions:** just before sunrise

The three dimensional nature of these clouds in a tropical sunrise, I leave to the imagination ...

Only a few pictures in my collection were taken without any planning, but spontaneous, by chance, a discovery. "Tropical Vibrance" is one of them.

I was working on a couple of ideas in Port Douglas, this time on the palm trees that line the northern end of Four Mile Beach. Arriving early and getting ready for the sunrise I was overwhelmed by the colour and the cloud formations of this rare and wonderful sunrise. So I left the palm trees and photographed ... **"Tropical Vibrance".**

This particular time as there were so many mosquitoes, I literally shot only three frames before being totally engulfed by them, they even chased me back to the car! From that day, insect repellent became an essential item in my kit.

"Then on the shore of the wide world
I stop and think till love and fame
To nothingness do sink"

John Keats, 1795-1821

"4 Mile Beach"
the township of Port Douglas, QLD

Perfect blue sky, perfect calm waters, perfectly still day; yet another perfect day in the tropics.

I miss small cameras, where I can play taking 'purely on the spur of the moment' photographs. This day was such a perfect day, so calm, so blue, and the water colour was lovely. So I decided to drop everything and spend the day doing just that. I drove up the coast stopping at all my favourite places, and captured ... "4 Mile Beach".

"Low Isles"
a tropical island, Port Douglas,

An island of paradise. A twenty minute boat trip from Port Douglas. Surrounded by coral reefs, where sailors anchor and spend a few days.

"4 Mile Beach"

Port Douglas, Far North Queensland

Film: 100ASA transparency   **Exposure:** 1/30 second   **Filtering:** polarised   **Time/conditions:** mid-day, perfect conditions

"Little Upolu"
One of three small sand cays situated off the coast of Cairns, Far North Queensland

Top: Green Island taken from water level showing the various coral formations and colour in the foreground.

Bottom: Green Island's north eastern side.

"Green Island"

A few kilometres off the coast of Cairns, Far North Queensland

A beautiful, picture perfect coral island in the Great Barrier Reef. Islands like Green Island form and build up over the years. Ocean currents and winds gather sand and form small sand cays. If conditions are right the sand continues to form. Birds making the cay their home deposit seeds and coconut palms also begin to take root. The vegetation attracts more life and assists in stabilising the sand. Depending on the environmental conditions, the newly formed island continues to grow or erodes away.

"Coral Sea"

From Rex Lookout, north of Cairns on the way to Port Douglas

The view from Rex Lookout is always spectacular regardless of the weather. But on a clear day, and there are many of those in Cairns, you can see for miles and the water is so calm it is awe inspiring.

Film: 100ASA transparency   **Exposure:** 1/4 second   **Filtering:** polarised   **Time/conditions:** mid-day, perfect conditions

"Cow Bay Beach"
Cape Tribulation, Far North Queensland

The beautiful calm tropical waters of the Tropical North; sitting under the cool shade of banyan trees, enjoying life.

I came across this wonderful location in the middle of a tropical rain, on one of my days out in search of a scene to photograph. Standing in the warm rain pondering the view, it felt like a deserted island. I felt like Robinson Crusoe. The tropical waters, the rain, the rainforest, with the sounds of the birds; what a wonderful place.

"Cow Bay" was photographed over a few weeks with several attempts to capture the atmosphere; the peacefulness, the calm waters, the blue sky and the shadows of the trees.

"Double Island"
Palm Cove, Ellis Beach North of Cairns

Tropical northern beaches have a particular charm that is unique to this part of the world. The Great Barrier Reef acts as a natural wall protecting these beautiful beaches. The waters are so often completely calm, with an inviting aqua colour, and the rainforest coming right to the sea and palm trees growing where they meet the water.

"There is only one success -
to be able to spend your life in your own way"

Christopher Morley

"Ellis Beach"

Ellis Beach north of Cairns, Far North Queensland

Film: 100ASA transparency   **Exposure:** 1/30 second   **Filtering:** polarised   **Time/conditions:** mid-day, perfect conditions

"Sand Cay"
Little Upolu sand cay 40km off the coast of Cairns, Far North Queensland

Film: 100ASA transparency   **Exposure:** 1/120th second   **Filtering:** polarised   **Time/conditions:** Perfect! Neap/calm tides, no wind

"Like an ocean flower
The island attracts the butterfly"

Tom MacPartland

Michiko patiently sat for 13 hours as I worked on this scene, though it looks like she just rolled up in her own plane, pulled on the hand brake for a quick dip and a time away from it all.

I had spent months preparing for this shot. In the middle of shooting I heard the sound of a light plane drawing closer and closer. Until it landed right in the middle of my perfect location. It proceeded then to turn around and park next to the sand cay.

I didn't know what to do except continue photographing. Later when I developed the film I was delighted. What a lovely expression of relaxation. Taking your own plane and just going wherever you like and what better place than your own beach in the middle of nowhere, and with a 360° view ... **"Sand Cay"**.

"Hook & Hardy Reef"
The Great Barrier Reef

Chosen for it's dramatic 120m deep channel that separates these two reefs. Coral in the foreground, a boat anchored and snorkellers swimming on the reef wall and more reefs on the horizon.

I worked on the idea of adding a reef scene to my collection for some time. The difference in capturing something fantastic at the reef compared to other scenes is it's relative inaccessibility. Also, I didn't want "just a photograph out of a plane", but then again the Great Barrier Reef is one of the 'Seven Wonders of the World' and by itself would be a wonder to photograph from the air. So I decided to work on two scenes: one from sea level "Little Upolu" and one from the air ... "Hook & Hardy".

I spent four hours flying around Hardy Reef at the Whitsundays, choosing this particular reef because of the dramatic channel that separates the two reefs. The channel is 120m deep, from the shallow coral to the ocean bed. Most of the time was spent flying in a plane around 5000 feet. With the door off, strapped in tightly, engine fumes and noise filling the cabin, it was freezing cold, nauseating and exhilarating.

"Knowledge is limited. Imagination encircles the whole world"

Albert Einstein

"The Great Reef"

The Great Barrier Reef, North Queensland

Film: 100ASA transparency   **Exposure:** 1/120th second   **Filtering:** polarised   **Time/conditions:** Perfect! Neap/calm tides, no wind

Film: 100ASA transparency   **Exposure:** 1/120th second   **Filtering:** polarised   **Time/conditions:** Perfect! Neap/calm tides, no wind

"Hook & Hardy Reef"
The Great Barrier Reef, North Queensland

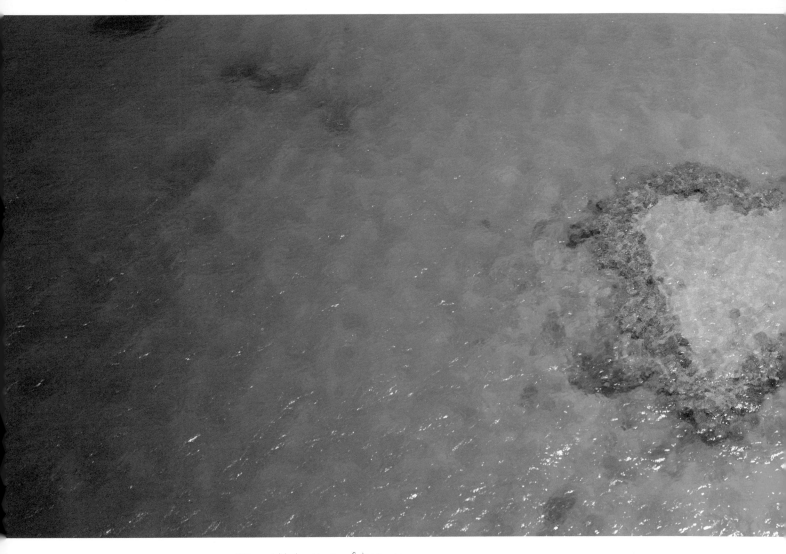

"For all lovers of beauty,
a Valentines card from Nature"

Tom MacPartland

"Heart Reef"
The Great Barrier Reef, North Queensland

"Whitehaven"

Whitehaven Beach, The Whitsunday Islands, North Queensland

Film: 100ASA transparency   **Exposure:** 1/120th second   **Filtering:** polarised   **Time/conditions:** Mid-day

Totally carefree, without a care in the world. With someone close, clear fresh air, a gentle breeze, puffy clouds and perfectly crystal clear waters.

We took a small Bell helicopter with floats where we could land right on this isolated beach. Flying low over the water and the islands, it felt as if we could almost reach out and touch the waves.

We landed right on the spot I had in mind. Leaving us with our gear, the helicopter took off to return a few hours later to pick us up.

Setting up on a small sand bar the tide was coming in so quickly, but I didn't mind for what a wonderful feeling; so totally carefree ... *"Whitehaven"*.

"The day, water, sun, moon, night -
I do not have to pay
to enjoy these things"

Platus, 254-184 BC

"Mossman" was captured with the full life and energy of this powerful river. With soft warm light, the huge boulders and the rainforest drawing you up to the 'Jurassic' like mountains in the distance.

I have spent a lot of time at Mossman Gorge, I always love it there. The river itself has an energy and life about it that is very special, so I decided to try to capture it in a frame.

I arrived around 6am, quickly finding a great vantage point, a large boulder in the middle of the river. It was unbelievable, the lighting was perfect; soft warm mauve light. I couldn't believe that everything could be so right on my first attempt, Until I started to make my way to the middle of the river. It was swollen. The water was over my shoulders and fast flowing. There was no way I could get to the vantage point with all my gear. So all I could do was watch until the light was gone.

I decided to return after purchasing a small rubber boat and waited for similar favourable conditions. The right lighting did not come again until the sixth visit, three weeks later. It was worth the wait ... *"Mossman"*.

"Mossman"

Mossman Gorge, Mossman Far North Queensland

Film: 100ASA transparency   **Exposure:** 1/4 second   **Filtering:** none   **Time/conditions:** Sunrise, with the sun reflecting off clouds to light the scene

"Eternal Fig"
A Fig Tree at Mossman Gorge, Mossman, Tropical North Queensland

Film: 100ASA transparency   **Exposure:** 2 minutes   **Filtering:** none   **Time/conditions:** 7am, just after rain

Previous page:

"Eternal Fig"
A Fig Tree at Mossman Gorge

"The Eternal Fig" has a wonderful angelic feel about it. With her branches reaching for the sky, ferns in her arms, warm sunlight and water still glistening from recent rains.

After many times hiking through this area, I was drawn to this magnificent tree by the roots that stretch like piping across the ground 50m in every direction. The tree seems to have her arms out-stretched to heaven, the queen of the forest with ferns as her royal subjects.

"The Eternal Fig" is the very first frame after 40 minutes of rain. Sunlight glistening everywhere, warm tones glowing in the warm light, and a fantastic heavenly glow of the sky due to the long exposure. Previous frames were exposed as long as 9 minutes - too long. And frames taken afterwards were marred by droplets on the lens that refused to dry.

It was a long time before I was brave enough to bring all my camera gear into the rain, but it was worth it. This was the seventh attempt to photograph this tree in three weeks of trying ... **"Eternal Fig"**.

"I think that I shall never see
A poem as lovely as a tree"

"Rainforest"
Mossman Gorge, Mossman, Tropical North Queensland

Film: 100ASA transparency   **Exposure:** 2 minutes   **Filtering:** none   **Time/conditions:** 7am, just after rain

"12 Apostles"
On The Great Ocean Road, Victoria

Film: 50ASA transparency   **Exposure:** 8 seconds   **Filtering:** none   **Time/conditions:** sunset

The great untouched land of Australia meeting the great unhindered open Southern Ocean. Hot red in the sunset, beautiful colours of the sandstone and the ocean.

The Great Ocean Road is on a fantastic stretch of coastline and the name of the road expresses the wonder of it. Situated west of Melbourne, the road covers lush green farmland with rolling hills, sandstone cliffs, rugged coastline and windswept land in the west.

I camped here for a number of days waiting for the sun to come out. Deciding not to wait any longer I travelled inland exploring Victoria a bit further. About a week later in the middle of the afternoon I noticed a clearing in the weather. Being only 200km from the 12 Apostles I made a dash for the sunset hoping to have a bit of clear sky on the horizon. The sun was beginning to be covered by cloud again but just before reaching the horizon it shone out in all it's glory ...

"12 Apostles".

A homestead in the mountains of Victoria used in the classic Australian movie, "The Man From Snowy River".

The Victorian mountains do amazing things for the soul, it is a wonder that not all Victorians own horses.

I camped near this location for six days whilst working on this photograph. Every morning and evening waiting for something special in the lighting. Though I loved every moment of it; the freshness of the air, the sounds of the birds, the silence, the Snow Gums, the peacefulness, the mountains and the view.

For all the hours that I was there the amount of times that I moved the camera because I felt that there was something wrong with the composition. Until the very last day, the composition came together, then the sun broke through the early morning clouds just enough to cast a warm light on the posts, the house. Not too strong, not too dark, a perfect balance ... *"Highlands".*

He is richest who is content with least, for contentment is the wealth of nature

Socrates, 468-399BC

"Highlands"

"The Man From Snowy River", Alpine Country, Victoria

Film: 50ASA transparency   **Exposure:** 2 minutes   **Filtering:** none   **Time/conditions:** sunrise, rain

The romance of the Snowy Mountains.

Two hours before this photograph was taken, large hail stones rained down on us for half an hour. Leaving us to cross a flooded mountain river, its icy water as low as 2° and the whole land was awash.

I had been looking for Snow Gums for some time, making several trips into the Snowy Mountains. Fortunately, I stumbled across this pair whilst trying to photograph the Blue Lakes on the opposite mountain range. A short time after discovering these trees the fog swept up the valley and over the ridge where we were, making the conditions perfect.

The first roll of film was grey, the next was yellow as the sun was setting and then changed to a soft magenta hue ... *"Snow Gums".*

"The branches turn, guided by Nature's love
The mist rolls in, connecting the lovers

Thus on a single branch the droplet is formed
A balance of what is new and what will be"

Paula Wilson

"Snow Gums"
Kosciuszko National Park, NSW

Film: 50ASA transparency **Exposure:** 2 minutes **Filtering:** none **Time/conditions:** sunset, fog

"A harmonious & intricate melody of Nature"   Nikola Ellery

Film: 50ASA transparency   **Exposure:** 20 minutes   **Filtering:** none   **Time/conditions:** early morning

"Kosciuszko Spring"
Upstream from Thredbo Village, Kosciuszko National Park NSW

"Fresh Awakening"

Bateman's Bay, South of Sydney

This area of Australia is particularly special with wild kangaroos and parrots that are tame enough to feed and secluded beaches, some of sand and others of smooth pebbles, and others still of coral and shells. I photographed this scene over a few months, trying to balance the high tide (needed for the waterfalls) with soft clouds to soften the sun's glow. I had already captured "Fresh Awakening" the day before, but I wanted to be sure. So I returned the next day early, set up to wait for the sunrise and just at the right (wrong) moment a freak wave crashed up washing the camera gear and us with 1000 litres of salt water ... fun.

Below right:

"Solitude"

A monument to the determination of man

Occasionally when there are very high clouds and the sun is setting, for only a few minutes the clouds turn a brilliant pink that lights up the whole landscape.

I had researched lighthouses for a few months, travelling to many of them. But this one was discovered quite by accident. I hiked out a dozen times before being fortunate to capture this one, quite unexpectedly and suddenly the light changed and a soft pink hue lightened up the whole scene and off on the right a storm front was moving in ... "Monument".

"Fresh Awakening"

Bateman's Bay, South of Sydney

Film: 50ASA transparency   **Exposure:** 8 seconds   **Filtering:** none   **Time/conditions:** sunrise & high tide

"Bach's Air on 'G'"
"Camel Rock" Bermagui, South of Sydney

Film: 50ASA transparency   **Exposure:** 1/2 second   **Filtering:** none   **Time/conditions:** sunrise

Australia's beaches; an appreciation for Australia's clear air, an endless love for the ocean and the peacefulness of first light.

When I was young I spent every holiday at this beach, it is a very special area for me.

I camped here for five days, only a few hundred metres from this scene, getting up early every morning in the hope of capturing something special in the lighting. For five days I worked on this scene, each day was clear and sunny, nothing exciting. But the fifth day brought some haze to soften the sun and a line of cloud to pick up the light ... **"Bach's Air on 'G'".**

"Love is the poetry
of the senses"

Honore De Balzac

"The tree, the sky, the water
The city, the Bridge, the Opera House
A combination of man and
Nature's creativity"

Tom MacPartland

Left:

"Good Morning Sydney"
Sunrise at Sydney Harbour, NSW

Sydney is one of the most wonderful cities in the world; with beautiful beaches, it's harbour, old sandstone architecture, the arts and the climate. Simply wonderful.

I have spent a lot of time in Sydney over the years, it is a great place to visit. There is so much to explore and experience. And when you travel out of town to the north, the south and the west the landscape is so varied, beautiful and dramatic. It is a photographer's paradise.

"Bondi Beach"
A beach in the middle of the city

"Breeze"

Halls Creek, 750km east of Broome Western Australia

One thing about driving around the Outback is the seemingly endless flat landscape. In a way it is like sailing on the open seas with all this open blue sky and continuous never changing scenery.

We had been driving thousands of kilometres over the last few days, without much change in the land, just the open horizon. Suddenly we came across some rolling hills that were completely covered with waist high grass. Like a dry oasis, something completely different - irresistible. So I had stop and have a good look around ... **"Breeze"**.

Film: 50 ASA transparency   **Exposure:** 1 second   **Filtering:** none   **Time/conditions:** sunset

www.steininger.com.au

Photography is a medium of formidable
contradictions - it is ridiculously easy
and impossibly difficult.

Edward Steichen (1879 - 1973)